SURVIVING WORLD WAR II AI

GW00319489

There are now more aircraft museums than ever before, and they are being visited by a happy combination of those who knew the aircraft in action and their descendants for whom these aircraft are part of living history.

This book is a concise guide to some of the World War II aircraft that can be seen in Britain, and contains photographs and descriptions of 30 aircraft that still survive. The favourites are here: the Hurricane (of which Douglas Bader led a squadron) and Spitfire fighters, the Lancaster bomber (which featured in the Dambusters raid led by Wing Commander Guy Gibson VC), the all-wood frame Mosquito bomber, the distinctive Sunderland flying boat, the American B-17 Fortress (best remembered for its important contribution to the 1943-45 daylight bombing offensive), the German Stuka and ME 109, and the only operational German World War II jet – the Messerschmitt 262. There are also interesting and more unusual aircraft, such as the Italian Fiat CR42, the Japanese Kawasaki Ki 100 and the British-built Boulton Paul Defiant – an aircraft without any forward-firing guns.

Included in each aircraft description are details of the speed, armaments, dates of service, area of operation and present location. The names and addresses of nearly 40 major aviation collections throughout the country are also given.

64 pages   30 colour photographs
List of aviation museums and collections

SURVIVING WORLD WAR II AIRCRAFT

CHAZ BOWYER

B. T. BATSFORD LTD, LONDON

First published 1981
© Chaz Bowyer 1981

ISBN 0 7134 3431 7

Set in ITC Zapf Book by Typewise Limited
Printed in Hong Kong
for the publishers, B. T. Batsford Ltd,
4 Fitzhardinge Street, London W1H 0AH

The Author and Publishers are grateful to the following for
supplying photographs: *R. Athey* pages 2-3, 11, 18-19, 20-21,
22-3, 26-7, 46-7, 48-9, 54-5; *Beaumont Aviation* pages 29, 32-3;
R. Bonser pages 58-9; *J. M. Bruce* pages 52-3; *Stuart Howe*
pages 7, 17, 30-31, 35, 36-7, 38, 40-41, 43, 50-51, 56; *RAF
Museum, Hendon* pages 8-9, 12-13, 14-15, 60-61; *R. Wright*
pages 24-5, 42, 45.

CONTENTS

The Aircraft

INTRODUCTION

The continuing enthusiasm for cherishing historic aircraft and associated paraphernalia is merely an extension of man's traditional regard for his past, stirred by an all-too-human emotion of pure nostalgia. If many of the men and women who created aviation history are no longer with us, then at least the aircraft in which they achieved fame can be kept for future generations to view and study. This book is intended simply to remind present and upcoming generations of existing historic aircraft – though merely a representative selection is actually featured herein – and to provide a broad reference listing of aeronautical collections which may be viewed in the United Kingdom at present. The particular aeroplanes described and illustrated here are all examples of machines flown during the war years 1939-45, but a host of other types of aircraft, both civil and military, from virtually every era of aviation history may also be seen at many of the museums and other collections listed.

Chaz Bowyer

AVRO 652A ANSON

Devised initially as a military variant of the six-seat civil passenger transport design, the Avro Anson first entered RAF operational service with 48 Squadron in March 1936. It was the first operational aircraft to incorporate a retractable undercarriage and, incidentally, the first monoplane type to be accepted for first-line use by the RAF under the expansion schemes of the late 1930s. Intended for coastal reconnaissance duties primarily, on the outbreak of war with Germany in September 1939 a total of 301 Ansons were on Coastal Command charge; nearly three times the total of all other aircraft types within the Command. During the first year of the war

Ansons gave a creditable account of themselves in attacking German shipping, U-boats and in occasional clashes with the Luftwaffe, but from late 1940 the design became one of the RAF's principal trainers and saw wide service also as a general communications 'hack'. Known to its many crews as 'Faithful Annie', the Anson lived up to its soubriquet by giving sterling service throughout the war, and the peace years, and production of the design finally ceased in May 1952, having totalled 11,020 Ansons of all types. The Anson was ultimately officially retired from RAF service in June 1968, thus terminating a longevity record of 32 years of faithful service.

The aircraft illustrated is an Anson XIX, a post-1945 transport variant (TX214), one of the reserve collection of the RAF Museum, Hendon, and pictured here at RAF Henlow.

AVRO 683 LANCASTER

Evolved originally in late 1939 as the Avro Manchester III, the Lancaster prototype, BT308, first flew on 9 January 1941, and by October of that year full production had commenced. Initial delivery to RAF operational service came in December 1941, when 44 Squadron began re-equipping with the type; and the first Lancaster war sorties were flown on 3 March 1942. On 17 April 1942 six Lancasters each from 44 and 97 Squadrons undertook a daring low-level daylight attack on a factory at Augsburg, and the formation leader, Sqn Ldr John Nettleton, was subsequently awarded the Victoria Cross, the first of ten Lancaster air crew members eventually awarded this highest gallantry decoration. From 1942 to the end of the European war, Lancasters figured largely in the Allied bombing offensive against Germany and Italy, and were responsible for many outstanding successes, including such epics as the Dambusters raid led by Wg Cdr Guy Gibson, VC, a daylight attack on Le Creusot, and the sinking of the German battleship *Tirpitz*. Successively modified in service, the Lancaster was capable of carrying the giant 12,000 lb *Tallboy* and 22,000 lb *Grand Slam* bombs, with which its crews achieved remarkable results in pure precision bombing raids. From 1942 to 1945 Lancasters flew a total of 156,000 operational sorties, and dropped some 609,000 tons of bombs. The type remained in RAF first-line service until replaced by its stable-mate design, the Avro Lincoln, and

9

the RAF's last Lancaster was eventually retired in October 1956.

Lancaster R5868 (illustrated), now on permanent display in the RAF Museum, Hendon, first entered service with 83 Squadron at Scampton and flew a total of 68 sorties as OL-Q-'Queenie'. After refurbishing, R5868 was then re-issued to 467 Squadron RAAF, coded PO-S 'Sugar', and completed an overall total of 135 sorties.

BOEING B-17 FORTRESS

Designed to meet a US Army requirement of 1934, the famous Boeing Fortress first flew in July 1935, and by 1941, when America declared war on Germany and Japan, more than 100 Fortresses were in service with the US Army Air Corps. Early versions of the type saw brief service with the RAF in mid-1941 but were not successful, though later modified variants saw extensive service with RAF Coastal Command in its anti-submarine offensive. The Fortress, however, is best remembered for its huge contribution to the daylight bombing offensive against Germany during the years 1943-45. Starting in August 1942, Fortress units of the US Eighth Air Force played an ever-increasingly important part in the Allied strategic bombing offensive, while the myriad of daylight battles with Luftwaffe fighters created a legend of courage and utter determination by the doughty Fortress crews. Continuously modified to carry more defensive armament, have greater range, and lift larger bomb loads, the B-17 continued in service with the USAF until 1960, some acting as air rescue aircraft during the Korean conflict. In all, some 12,731 Fortresses were built throughout the aircraft's life-span, and its operational strength with the American air forces reached its peak in August 1944, when a total of 4574 B-17s were on USAF charge. By VE-Day ('Victory in Europe') Fortresses had dropped 640,000 tons of bombs during a total of 291,508 operational missions; while B-17 gunners had claimed some 6600 aerial victories.

The Fortress illustrated here is a B-17G version, built in 1945 and originally serialled 44-85784, now on charge of Duxford, where it regularly flies for public display purposes.

BOULTON PAUL DEFIANT

Designed to a 1935 Air Ministry Specification, the Boulton Paul Defiant two-seat fighter first flew in prototype form on 11 August 1937. The first RAF fighter in squadron use to have a four-gun power-operated turret, the Defiant was originally intended to combat enemy bomber formations by flying on the beam of the bombers and employing its turret armament accordingly; thus no forward-firing guns were fitted into its wings or fuselage. Initially equipping 264 Squadron in December 1939, Defiants first saw action in May 1940. After some early successes in combat, however, Defiant losses mounted swiftly and the type was withdrawn from day use and relegated to night fighting and other roles. Later still Defiants saw relatively wide service in the air-sea rescue units and as target-towing trainer aircraft. In all, 30 squadrons were Defiant-equipped; the total production of 1064 aircraft ended in February 1943.

Seen here is Defiant N1671, painted in the wartime markings of 307 (Polish) Squadron and on permanent display at the RAF Museum at Hendon. It first joined 307 Squadron on 17 September 1940 at Kirton-in-Lindsey, Lincolnshire, with which unit it saw brief operational use as a night fighter. Later serving with 153 and 285 (ASR) Squadrons, N1671 was struck off RAF charge on 21 June 1947, only to be refurbished to its present state by 19 Maintenance Unit at St Athan 20 years later, and moved to the RAF Museum.

BRISTOL BEAUFIGHTER

Designed originally as a private venture, high performance, long-range fighter by revamping the Bristol Beaufort, the Bristol Type 156 Beaufighter prototype (R2052) was completed by July 1939 and was immediately adopted by the Air Ministry and ordered for production for the RAF. The first production example to be issued to the RAF was delivered to Tangmere on 12 August 1940, and Beaufighter operations commenced slowly from 4 September 1940. With a maximum speed well in excess of 300 mph, and (eventually) standard armament comprising four 20 mm cannons in the fuselage, plus six .303 machine guns in the wings, the Beaufighter became the most powerfully armed fighter employed by the RAF throughout World War II. This battery of guns was later complemented by eight three-inch rocket projectiles carried under the wings, while one variant was adapted to carry a 1650 lb or 2127 lb torpedo, and others were fitted with carriers for various 250 lb and/or 500 lb bombs. After initial use as a nightfighter, Beaufighters were issued to Coastal Command for anti-shipping operations; and from May 1941 were introduced to the desert air war in North Africa. By December 1941 Beaufighters had begun operations in India and Burma, and the deadly reputation of the Beau led to its nickname 'Whispering Death' in this theatre of operations. Before the final production Beaufighter was delivered in September 1945, a total of more than

5500 aircraft were built, while a further 364 were manufactured locally in Australia to supplement the 217 Beaus transferred (ex-RAF) to the RAAF. The last Beau in RAF service (a TTX, RD761) made its last flight on 12 May 1960 from Seletar, Singapore.

Photo shows Beaufighter TTX, RD253, at the RAF Museum, Hendon. Built in 1944, this Beau was sold to the Portuguese Navy in March 1945, and was given back to the RAF circa 1965. After complete refurbishment by RAF St Athan, it was handed over to the RAF Museum in March 1971.

CHANCE VOUGHT CORSAIR

With its distinctive inverted gull-wing, the Corsair fighter was conceived in mid-1938 for eventual use by the US Navy, and made its first flight in May 1940. First production Corsairs began to come from the factories in June 1942, and these had their operational debut in US service in February 1943 at Guadalcanal with US Marine Corps Squadron VMF 124. By the end of that year Corsair pilots had claimed 584 victories in combat with Japanese aircraft. In June 1943 the first British Fleet Air Arm unit to be equipped with Corsairs was 1830 Squadron, FAA, which was formed and trained in America, and eventually at least 19 FAA squadrons used Corsairs during the war. FAA Corsairs first flew operationally in April 1944, mainly from British aircraft carriers in European waters, and proved to be formidable weapons in the naval air armoury. Armed with four wing-mounted .50-inch calibre machine guns, and often fitted with up to 2000 lb of bombs, the Corsair could still achieve speeds in excess of 360 mph, with a high degree of manoeuvrability. In terms of FAA operations, the Corsair was particularly prominent in the Pacific zone of operations during 1944-45, attacking a wide variety of sea and land targets, and accounting for many Japanese aircraft in combat. It was in a Corsair – FG-1D, KD658 of 1841 Squadron, FAA from *HMS Formidable* – that Lt Robert H Gray, DSC, of the RCNVR earned the last air VC ever awarded.

Leading a Corsair strike force on 9 August 1945 against Japanese shipping, Gray was killed in action, only six days before peace was declared. The Corsair continued in production for the US Navy and USMC until December 1952, by which time a total of 12,571 aircraft had been built, and the last Corsairs to see operational action were a handful involved in the French Indo-China conflict.

CONSOLIDATED B-24 LIBERATOR

Together with the Boeing B-17 Fortress, the B-24 Liberator was the backbone of the USAAF strategic bombing offensive against Germany in the years 1943-45, while in RAF use the Liberator saw wide and invaluable service in the Middle and Far East theatres of war, and especially in Coastal Command in an anti-submarine role. Designed to a US Army specification of 1939, the B-24 was the first American heavy bomber to incorporate a tricycle undercarriage, while its very slim, high aspect ratio Davis wings, a new conception in wing design, offered extremely long range; an asset which was to be put to important use on operations. Of the earliest batch to be produced, 120 were ordered by the French, but in 1940 this order was taken over by the RAF, and the first RAF Liberator (AM258) first flew in January 1941, and within months others were being ferried across the Atlantic to the UK. Some of these entered Coastal Command from September 1941, and continued in use against German submarines until the end of the war;

claiming almost a third of all U-boats sunk or damaged by Allied aircraft throughout the war. The RAF also used the Liberator extensively as a heavy bomber, mainly in the overseas war zones, particularly in Burma where, from January 1944, it was the principal long-range 'heavy' in RAF use. Elsewhere, converted and modified Liberators were used as transport and freight carriers. With the USAAF, the B-24 commenced operations with the Eighth Air Force in Britain on 9 October 1942, and thereafter played an increasingly large part in USAAF bombing missions. In terms of altitude, bomb load carried, speed, and all-round efficiency, the B-24 was superior to the famed B-17 Fortress, and Liberators were built in greater numbers than any other US military aircraft in World War II, of which nearly 2500 were used by the RAF or its Commonwealth air forces.

The example shown here was last located at Duxford.

De HAVILLAND MOSQUITO

Another classic aircraft which was first envisaged as a private venture design before the Air Ministry expressed interest was the De Havilland 98 Mosquito. First planned in October 1938, it was not until early 1940 that officialdom placed a production order. Of all-wood construction, carrying no defensive armament, the initial design was intended to rely on pure speed to avoid interception. The first prototype (W4050) made its first flight on 25 November 1940 and immediately demonstrated its near-400 mph speed, combined with astonishing fluid manoeuvrability for an intended bomber design. Entering RAF service originally with the Photographic Development Unit, Benson, the first bomber versions were issued to 105 Squadron at Swanton Morley, Norfolk, in November 1941, and commenced operations in the latter role on 31 May 1942. Produced in a variety of military variants, Mosquitos soon began to replace Beaufighters in the nightfighter role, and supplement RAF Bomber Command's night bombing offensive. Flying sorties by day or night, Mosquito crews quickly established an unsurpassed reputation for precision attacks on individual targets, leading eventually to their employment with the Path Finder Force (8 Group) and 5 Group as target finders and markers for the heavy bomber streams. By 1944, Mosquitos were also replacing Beaufighters in Coastal Command as anti-shipping strike bombers, while several squadrons of Fighter Command were specialising in night fighter escort and intruder roles, roaming the night skies of Germany and creating havoc among the Luftwaffe's night defenders. Several Mosquito squadrons saw service in the Middle and Far East theatres of war, though in relatively small quantities. Total Mosquito production throughout the British Empire amounted to 7781 aircraft. The last example in RAF service, a PR34A, RG314, made the ultimate RAF operational sortie on 15 December 1955 from its base in Seletar, Singapore.

The aircraft illustrated was marked in spurious

RAF codings for the 1968 film *Mosquito Squadron*, but examples of other Mosquitos may be found in several UK air museums, especially the Mosquito Aircraft Museum at Salisbury Hall, London Colney which contains the original prototype among others.

De HAVILLAND 82 TIGER MOTH

Developed from the popular De Havilland Gipsy Moth, the Tiger Moth first flew in prototype form in October 1931 and entered RAF service as an

elementary trainer in February 1932. It was to remain in active use by the RAF for the next 15 years and, in the event, became the RAF's last biplane trainer. During those years Tiger Moths trained more RAF pilots than any other aircraft designed for such a purpose. Fully aerobatic, and powered by a 120 hp Gipsy III (Mk 1) or 130 hp Gipsy Major engine (Mk 2), the Tiger Moth endeared itself to all its crews, and an overall total in excess of 8800 were built, including 3328 in Canada, Australia, New Zealand, Norway, Sweden and Portugal. Apart from its prime role as a trainer, a number of Tiger Moths saw active service with Coastal Command during the opening months of World War II as submarine 'hunters', patrolling UK coastal waters acting as 'spotters' for the RAF and Royal Navy. One interesting experiment involving Tiger Moths was the testing and production of 420 aircraft as 'Queen Bees', radio-controlled anti-aircraft 'targets' which flew without crews, being controlled from the ground. First flown in this guise on 5 January 1935, the 'Queen Bee' came in both landplane and floatplane configurations. Even after being phased out of RAF service, Tiger Moths remained popular with civil flying enthusiasts, and in 1956 the Tiger Club was formed to perpetuate the Tiger Moth and inaugurate a regular formation for 'Tigers' to participate in aerial displays and other private functions, a service still very much in existence and active.

The example illustrated, DF130, is doped in typical wartime camouflage and other markings. The aircraft are still fairly plentiful, and can be seen at Duxford, Yeovilton, Hendon and other locations.

DOUGLAS DAKOTA

Indisputably the most famous of all RAF transport aircraft, the Dakota – or 'Dak' as it was commonly called – saw war service in every known zone of operations by the RAF and the American air services during 1939-45. A militarised version of the highly successful Douglas DC3 civil transport, Dakotas (the RAF title) served with the RAF from 1941 until the final flight by a Dakota bearing RAF roundels on 1 April 1970 – an almost unprecedented record of loyal and patient service. Nearly 2000 Dakotas were supplied to the RAF, which employed it as transport, freight, paratroop, general communications and, occasionally, VIP vehicle. Powered by twin 1200 hp Pratt and Whitney Twin Wasp engines, a Dakota I could lift 28 fully armed troops and a three-man crew, or, as in India and

Burma, a bewildering variety of military stores, including mules. In the Far East war theatre Dakotas were the lynch-pin of Brigadier-General Orde Wingate's Chindit columns, who fought hundreds of miles behind Japanese lines and relied entirely upon the Daks to deliver all their supplies from the air. Elsewhere during the war Dakotas operated as pure freights, as over Arnhem in September 1944, when a Dakota captain of 271 Squadron, Flt Lt David Lord, DFC, died attempting to deliver fresh ammunition supplies to beseiged paratroops despite a fire in one of his Dakota's engines. Lord was awarded a posthumous Victoria Cross – the only VC ever awarded to a transport pilot. Other wartime uses included ambulance work and glider-towing during the invasion of France in 1944-45. After the war Dakotas played an important role in the initial stages of the Berlin Airlift; while in the early 1950s Dakotas were used in the anti-terrorist campaign ('Operation Firedog') in Malaya as 'sky-speakers'; fitted with loudspeakers and voicing propaganda to the Communist 'bandits' in the jungle.

The Dakota here, painted as KG374, the identity of Flt Lt D Lord, VC's aircraft, is in reality KN645, which was handed over to the RAF in May 1945 and saw extensive service with the RAF, before finally finding a permanent home at its present location, the RAF Cosford Aerospace Museum, near Wolverhampton.

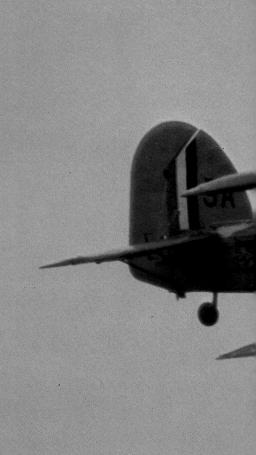

FAIREY SWORDFISH

The Fairey Swordfish – or 'Stringbag' as it was affectionately dubbed by all its crews – is almost legendary in Fleet Air Arm annals. Obsolete by all normal standards at the outbreak of war in 1939 – it had been designed in 1932 – with vintage appearance and characteristics, the Swordfish nevertheless served operationally throughout World War II and established for itself a fighting record second to none in its own roles. Its popularity lay in its superb handling qualities, which made it almost the ideal aircraft for aircraft

carrier operations and torpedo work. Entering FAA service with 825 Squadron in July 1936, Swordfish eventually equipped a total of 25 squadrons, while its total production of 2391 aircraft only ceased in December 1944. Its fighting record commenced on 13 April 1940 during the Norwegian campaign when a Swordfish from *HMS Warspite* sank the German submarine U-64, the first U-boat to be destroyed by an FAA aircraft. Thereafter Swordfish were prominent in virtually every naval engagement, reaching a peak of success on the night of 11 November 1940, when a total force of 21 Swordfish attacked the Italian Fleet at Taranto and effectively crippled it, thereby altering the balance of naval power at sea. Elsewhere in the Mediterranean zone Swordfish based on Malta created havoc among enemy shipping lanes supplying the German Afrika Korps from 1940 to 1942; others aboard the *Ark Royal* participated in preventing the use of the French Fleet by the Vichy French. Perhaps the best-remembered epic of courage associated with the Swordfish was, ironically, one of its few failures, when, on 12 February 1942, Lt-Cdr Eugene Esmonde, DSO, led a formation of six 825 Squadron aircraft in a courageous but vain attempt to torpedo the German capital ships *Scharnhorst*, *Gneisenau* and *Prinz Eugen* in the English Channel. All six aircraft were lost, with only five crew members surviving. Esmonde was awarded a posthumous Victoria Cross.

Illustrated is LS326, built in 1943 and retained by the FAA Museum at Yeovilton, which continues to be flown at air displays – the sole airworthy example of a proud fighting breed.

FIAT CR42

Produced in 1939 as a development of the Fiat CR32 fighter which saw service in the Spanish Civil War, the CR42 Freccia ('Arrow') was designed by Ing. Rosatelli, and used much of its predecessor's style of construction, including the Warren-bracing of the wings which substituted for more normal flying and landing wires. Its 840 hp engine gave it a top speed in the region of 270 mph, and its armament comprised either two or four 12.7 mm machine guns. As the couterpart of the RAF's Gloster Gladiator, it was obsolete for the warfare standards of 1940-45, but during its main operational service in East and North Africa the CR42, in intelligent hands, was highly manoeuvrable and not unsuccessful against more modern monoplane opponents. Of all-metal construction with fabric covering for the wings, a total of 1800 CR42s were eventually built, the last of these as late as 1942. In the North African campaign CR42 squadrons were handicapped more by a lack of supplies to

maintain the aircraft than the admittedly out-
dated performance of the machines, and at one
period some units were reduced to just three
serviceable aircraft fit for operations. In combat
the CR42's extreme aerobatic qualities more often
saved its pilots than gained success, and by 1942
the type was withdrawn from fighter operations.

A few were then modified to carry two 220lb
bombs for close support duties with the army,
and experimental versions were built with either
retractable undercarriage or twin floats, but
neither achieved production status.

The example illustrated is now with the RAF
Museum, Hendon.

FOCKE WULF Fw 190

Custom-built and designed with the needs of both operational fighting, flying and ground maintenance uppermost in mind, the Focke Wulf Fw 190 – brainchild of Kurt Tank – came near to being the ideal fighter design of World War II. Simplicity in all things, combined with superb manoeuvrability, speed and control, gave the first Fw 190 pilots an immediate superiority over all existing Allied fighters when it was introduced to the air war in July 1941. The prototype first flew on 1 June 1939, and by the early summer of 1941 the first 100 production examples were under service testing. The Fw 190 first flew in action in July with JG 26, commanded by Adolf Galland, based on the French coast. Its patent superiority over the RAF's latest Mk V Spitfire gave the Luftwaffe local aerial supremacy for many months ahead. As with every operational aircraft ever built, the Fw 190 was subject to a continuous programme of modification and improvement in the light of operational needs, with improved engine power, more powerful armament, and adaption as a low-level fighter-bomber or dive-bomber. By mid-1943 Fw 190s were also being employed as freelance night fighters, using the *Wilde Sau* ('Wild Boar') tactics then in vogue, but although initially successful the losses among Fw 190 pilots rose alarmingly by the end of the year and the type reverted to its day role. By 1944 development of the basic design produced a series of high altitude variants, incorporating pressurised

cockpit cabins and up-rated engines; while the most significant version to appear next was the Fw 190D-series, with much-extended fuselage and engine housing – these being dubbed 'Long-nose' by their opponents. The Fw 190D could reach speeds of 440 mph with ease, yet still retained the type's superb control behaviour. The ultimate variant to be built before the end of the war was the Fw 190 known as the Ta152H-1; a 'stretched' design which could outpace in speed and climb any Allied fighter in operational use then.

More than 20,000 Fw 190s were finally built, and the example illustrated is an Fw 190A-8/U1 two-seater, at present owned by the RAF Museum, Hendon.

GLOSTER GLADIATOR

Last of a long line of RAF biplane fighters to see active service, the Gloster Gladiator flew in its prototype form initially in September 1934, and entered RAF service in production form in February 1937, with 72 Squadron as the first unit to be fully re-equipped with the type. Armed with four .303-inch calibre machine guns, and capable of a top speed of about 250 mph, the Gladiator virtually introduced RAF fighter pilots of the day to enclosed cockpits. Though eventually to equip a total of 36 squadrons or other units, the bulk of these had been replaced by more modern aircraft before the outbreak of war, and on 1 September 1939 the RAF possessed a total of 218 Gladiators, with only 76 of these on the strength of Fighter Command. Two squadrons, 607 and 615 AAF, saw brief operational service in France during the opening months of the war, but the Gladiators' first real testing came in the disastrous Norwegian campaign in early 1940. Against vastly superior odds, including climatic conditions, a handful of Gladiators fought gallantly but in vain. Similar odds were encountered in the Greek campaign, where the RAF's highest-scoring fighter ace of World War II, Sqn Ldr 'Pat' Pattle, accomplished many of his victories from a Gladiator cockpit. In Malta a few Gladiators helped repel some of the initial air assaults by the Axis air forces, while the early campaigns in the Western Desert of North Africa saw Gladiators in frontline action.

Today, the only surviving airworthy example is L8032 (illustrated) belonging to the Shuttleworth

Collection at Old Warden, Bedfordshire. Built originally in 1937, it saw wartime service, and in the postwar years passed through various owners before being presented to the Shuttleworth Trust in November 1960. It is marked in the pre-1939 colours of 72 Squadron.

HAWKER HURRICANE

The introduction of the Hawker Hurricane to RAF squadrons ushered in a new era in fighter design, being the first eight-gun monoplane in operational use, and the RAF's first fighter capable of exceeding 300 mph with a full war load. As with several other classic designs to be employed by the RAF, the Hurricane was originally a private venture design, by Sydney Camm of Hawkers, beginning in October 1933. In February 1935 an Air Ministry contract was awarded for the construction of one prototype, which first flew on 6 November 1935, to be followed in June 1936 by a further contract for 600 machines. The Hurricane first entered RAF use with 111 Squadron at Northolt in December 1937, and by September 1939 the RAF had a total of 18 squadrons equipped with the type; twice the total of Spitfire units. The hard-working Hurricane bore the brunt of aerial combat in France until mid-1940, and throughout the ensuing Battle of Britain was the mainstay of Fighter Command. The national debt owed to the Hurricane during the crucial 1940 battles can be exemplified by the simple facts that more Hurricanes were flown than *all* other types combined, and Hurricane pilots accounted for almost 80 per cent of all victories achieved or claimed. In the following war years 1941-45, Hurricanes continued to give splendid service in every possible theatre of operations, and being flown in virtually every possible role for a single-engined fighter. Total production of Hurricanes of all types amounted to 14,231, with British production ceasing in September 1944. Today several flying examples are maintained and displayed, including machines of the RAF's Battle of Britain Flight.

The example illustrated is LF363 (see pages 2-3), marked in the code letters of 242 Squadron when the unit was based at RAF Coltishall in mid-1940, commanded by Sqn Ldr Douglas Bader, DSO, DFC.

HEINKEL He 162

The Heinkel He 162 *Volksjäger* ('People's Fighter') was a prime example of the desperate steps taken in Germany to avert defeat in the final months of World War II. Its conception came from a conference held in September 1944 calling for a defensive fighter which could be simply produced and quickly, using semi-skilled labour and readily-available materials. From the various designs offered by different manufacturers, the Heinkel He 162 was accepted. Within the following 90 days the first example was ready –

an astonishing tribute to the unceasing energy and dedication of its designers and constructors. Ordered into immediate production at a projected output of 1000 He 162s per month, the first example made its maiden flight on 6 December 1944, and its BMW *Sturm* axial flow turbo-jet engine gave it a top speed of 522 mph during this 20-minute trial. Only four days later the pilot was killed when the aircraft broke up in a low-level run. Production continued unabated of the tiny metal-fuselage, wooden-winged interceptor, and the first operational unit equipped was JG 84, based at Leck. At least 116 He 162s were actually built before the war in

Europe ceased, and apart from one or two isolated sorties, none of these saw action. An indication of the pure fantasy world in which the contemporary German hierarchy lived can be seen by the fact that the Luftwaffe commander, Hermann Göring, originally believed that the He 162 could easily be flown by thousands of the Hitler Youth movement after simple 'conversion' from glider training . . . .

Illustrated is He 162A-1 *'Salamander'* 120235 which served with 1/JG 1 when captured at Leck in May 1945. It now belongs to the Imperial War Museum, London.

JUNKERS Ju 52/3m

The principal workhorse of the Luftwaffe throughout its existence, the Junkers Ju 52 – known universally at *Tante Ju* ('Auntie Ju') – was developed from the single-engined Ju 52 of 1930, and first flew in its tri-motor form in April 1932. Angular and highly functional in outline, it employed the Junkers corrugated metal wing and fuselage skin, and in 1932 first went into use as a commercial transport, 15-seat airliner with Lufthansa. In this guise it was to be employed ultimately by some 30 countries. Two years later a militarised version was produced for the then secret Luftwaffe, intended as a heavy *(sic)* bomber, and it entered military service initially in 1935 with *Kampfgeschwader* 152 'Hindenburg'. Its career as a pure bomber was, however, fairly brief, and only a few saw such service in the Spanish Civil War. In 1937 its main task was changed to pure transport duties. By September 1939 the Luftwaffe possessed well over 500 Ju 52s, and the type first made its mark on operations as a paratroop carrier, a task it was to be used for successfully for several years, particularly in the Norwegian, Greek, Crete and other campaigns. Due to its low performance range, the Ju 52 suffered heavily in each of these assaults – the Crete invasion alone cost the Luftwaffe more than 170 Ju 52s shot down, with more than 7000 troops killed or wounded – and this vulnerability to ground fire was to lead to the type's exclusive use as a transport and freight carrier after 1942. Even in this role casualties among the Ju 52 *Gruppen* continued to reach alarming figures, an

example being the re-supply of German forces surrounded at Demyansk. In three months of unceasing operations here, 262 aircraft were lost. At Stalingrad, nearly half of the 400 Ju 52s used to relieve encircled German troops were destroyed

or lost on operations in just eight weeks. In the Mediterranean zone no less than 432 German transports were shot down by Allied fighters in a mere three weeks, as the aged Ju 52s attempted to fly fuel and supplies to Rommel's Afrika Korps.

In all, some 5000 Ju 52s were actually built, and in the immediate post-war years a number of survivors continued to fly as civil transports with various countries until circa 1950.

JUNKERS Ju 87
STUKA

The Junkers Ju 87 is a prime example of how an aircraft could gain international notoriety of almost legendary proportions, yet remain in essence a design obsolete and highly vulnerable for its appointed operational tasks. Of distinctly ugly appearance, the original concept was as a dive-bomber; hence the incorporation of full-span dive brakes and flaps in the wings, and the separated undercarriage housings in order to facilitate carriage of bombs under the main fuselage. Design commenced in 1934, and the first prototype was flight-tested by the end of 1935. Production aircraft began being delivered to the recently created Luftwaffe in early 1937; the first Ju 87 unit being *Sturzkampfgeschwader Immelmann.* In December 1937 three examples were despatched to Spain to join the German Condor Legion, and these went into action initially to test the capability of such a dive-bomber under actual war conditions. Used for attacking specific 'spot' targets such as road and rail junctions, bridges, ships and individual ground installations, the Ju 87 proved highly successful. Its fame was enlarged during the opening phases of the European war in 1939-40, when the Ju 87 became a form of forward artillery for the army, and pure bomber. The soubriquet *Stuka* – a semi-mnemonic for *Sturzkampfflugzeug* – became allied to the Ju 87, and it gained a fearsome reputation. The subsequent Battle of Britain, however, swiftly dispelled this unearned notoriety, when RAF fighters massacred the Ju 87 formations despatched to attack Britain. From 1941 the Ju 87 reverted to its prime role of close support for the army, and gained a formidable reputation as a tank-killer on the Russian front, while in other war zones its dive-bombing accuracy still offered successes in an anti-shipping role.

In design ugly to the point of absurdity, and easy prey for any determined fighter opposition, the Ju 87 gained a false reputation for its prowess and cost the lives of hundreds of faithful crews, yet its name remains probably one of the best-remembered of German wartime bombers.

The Ju 87D-3/Trop pictured (No. 494085, 'W8-AE') is part of the reserve collection of the RAF Museum, viewed here at RAF St Athan.

JUNKERS Ju 88

Produced in greater quantities than all other German bombers combined, the Junkers Ju 88 was also the subject of the most intensive and variable modification throughout the war of 1939-45. More than 15,000 Ju 88s were built, some 9000 of these as bombers and the bulk of the remainder as fighters. Its original design began in January 1936, and the prototype first flew in December of that year. Modification programmes immediately inaugurated resulted in major engine changes and overall design features, and despite slow production deliveries

in the early stages, the Ju 88 made its first operational sorties over Scotland in September 1939. Production gained momentum in 1940 and Ju 88s participated in strength during the Battle of Britain, while the following year tropicalized versions were introduced to the North African zone of war. In 1941 too Ju 88s first figured in the German assault on Russia, where major armament modifications permitted its use as a low-level close support aircraft, tackling tanks and ground installations. Conversions of the basic Ju 88 to a pure fighter role began relatively early in the war, and by 1943-44 many of the German night fighter units were equipped with cannon-armed, radar-carrying Ju 88s in the pure interception role. Other major versions to be introduced were pure reconnaissance variants, involving drastic redesign of the forward crew cabin and main wings; as torpedo bomber, VIP transport, high altitude bomber, photo reconnaissance, and other minor tasks. In many of these roles, the aircraft title was successively altered to Ju 188, Ju 288, Ju 388 and so on. The ultimate war use for the Ju 88 was as a pilotless missile, whereby the fuselage was altered to become simply a container for a hollow-charge warhead, with all flight controls operated from a Messerschmitt Bf 109 or Focke Wulf Fw 190 mounted above – the so-termed *Mistel* combination 'aircraft'. Despite its extensive adaption and redesigning to meet the myriad urgently needed operational requirements of the Luftwaffe, the Ju 88 remains the finest bomber design produced by Germany during 1938-45.

The RAF Museum at Hendon has an aircraft on display.

KAWASAKI Ki 100

Though only met in action during the closing months of the Pacific war in early 1945, the Kawasaki Ki 100 immediately proved itself to be possibly the best fighter produced for the Japanese air services in the war. Its origins were virtually accidental, being a last-minute idea for re-engining the already successful Kawasaki Ki 61 *Hien* – code-named 'Tony' by the Allies – which has been the standard Japanese Army Air Force fighter of the 1943-44 period. By the end of 1944 a serious shortage of the Ha 40 in-line engines required for the *Hien* ('Flying Swallow')

necessitated hasty experimentation with the only other reliable – and available in quantity – powerplant; the Mitsubishi Ha 112-II 14-cylinder air-cooled radial. By modifying the engine housing, the new, bigger engine was fitted into existing Ki 61 airframes, and the first 'conversion' flew on 1 February 1945. Testing produced surprisingly favourable results – the new configuration was undoubtedly far superior to its 'parent', and production was ordered immediately. USAAF bombing raids were responsible for destroying the factories producing the new fighter, but the relatively few Ki 100s to enter operational service quickly established their fighting potential by destroying

14 Grumman F6F Hellcat fighters over Okinawa in a single combat, without Japanese loss. Simple to fly and easy to maintain, the Ki 100 was popular with Japanese pilots and ground crews, and only the end of the war prevented the use of a much-improved version which would have been capable of tackling American B-29 Superfortresses at their usual high altitude.

The example pictured here at RAF Cosford's Aerospace Museum is a Ki 61 which had been converted to Ki 100 standards, captured in 1945, and displayed in the colour markings of the Japanese 5th Fighter Squadron. It has an Ha 112-71 radial engine.

MESSERSCHMITT Bf 109

With the distinction of being manufactured in larger quantity than *any* other operational aircraft of World War II, of any nation, the Messerschmitt Bf 109 fighter was the standard German fighter for nearly a decade, with a total production figure in excess of 33,000 aircraft of all versions. Conceived in mid-1934, the first prototype was powered by a Rolls Royce Kestrel V engine, and first flew in the summer of 1935. In modified form (including replacement of the Kestrel with a

Junkers Jumo engine), the first examples for service evaluation went to the reformed *Richthofen Jagdgeschwader* in 1937; and in July that year 24 Bf 109 of JG I/88 in Spain tested the design under actual war conditions. Further improvement in armament and engine power led eventually to the Bf 109E version, the first true mass-production model of the design, and by 1940 the E-variant had replaced all previous versions in service with the Luftwaffe. It was with the Bf 109E that German fighter pilots fought the RAF and the Allied air forces during 1939-40, including the Battle of Britain operations. In January 1941 an improved, more powerful model, the Bf 109F, began reaching first-line units and by the summer was in wide use. The only other significant variant to reach wide operational use was the Bf 109G, which commenced delivery from the factories late in 1942. The G-variant – known as the *'Gustav'* to its crews – accounted for almost 70 per cent of total Bf 109 production during the war years; from which flowed a wide variety of day or night fighters, high altitude reconnaissance and, occasionally, two-seat operational trainers. Armament varied considerably on occasion, including underwing pods for rockets, bombs, heavy cannons *et al*, while night fighter versions were fitted with radar warning and homing apparatus for tackling the increasing menace of Allied heavy bombers over the Reich. Throughout the war virtually every top-scoring German fighter pilot flew the Bf 109, while Major Erich Hartmann, whose confirmed tally of 352 victories made him the all-time 'Ace of Aces' of the world, flew nothing but Bf 109s during his fighting career.

The Bf 109E-3 illustrated belonged to *Staffel 2* of JG51 at Wissant when, on 27 November 1940, its pilot Wolfgang Teumer, was forced to land at Manston. Today it belongs to the RAF Museum, Hendon.

MESSERSCHMITT Me 262

The history of the Me 262 twin-jet fighter is a prime example of lack of decision by the Luftwaffe hierarchy and, hence, lost opportunity. Radical in design, and with huge potential in its original conception as a fighter, the Me 262 was finally used in insufficient quantity and too late to have the full impact on the European aerial conflict that it might have had if it had been put into full service when it first became available to the Luftwaffe. Envisaged initially in late 1938 as 'Projekt 1065', the preliminary design was completed by June 1939, and in March 1940 construction of three prototypes began. These were completed by April 1941, in which month the first flights were made. Nevertheless, officialdom gave the project a low priority, and its further development was undertaken privately by the Messerschmitt design team. It was not until October 1942 that a tentative production order was placed with the factory, for just 15 aircraft. Testing and improvement continued at the manufacturers despite official apathy, until Adolf Galland finally brought pressure to bear on his superiors and a full production order was granted in July 1943, only to be reversed on the personal order of Adolf Hitler. Four months later Hitler relented but insisted the design be adapted as a fast bomber, and he forbade its development a a fighter! Only in March 1945 was this order finally rescinded and Me 262 fighter units went into action – though in its so-termed 'bomber' role the Me 262 had first become operational with KG51 in late 1944. The potential of the fighter version may be judged by one interception sortie on 7 April 1945, when JV44 attacked a formation of B-17 Fortresses and destroyed 25 of these within minutes. The Me 262's technical advantages and huge superiority over all other operational fighters could quite possibly have changed the whole course of the air war had it been adopted in 1942-43. Instead the design was to suffer a brief and, in the event, unproductive career.

The photo shows Me 262A-2a of 1/KG51, though fitted with wings from another Me 262, at present held on the charge of the RAF Cosford Aerospace Museum.

NORTH AMERICAN MITCHELL

Manufactured in larger quantities than any other American twin-engined bomber – a total of 9816 aircraft – the Mitchell, named after the crusading visionary of air power, General 'Billy' Mitchell, USAAC, saw service with every Allied air service in World War II. Indeed, only just over a quarter of its production total was actually used by the American air forces, the rest going to British, Soviet and other allies. Known as the B-25 to the USAAF, the Mitchell's origins derived from a 1938 US Army specification, and, as the NA-40-1 Attack Bomber, the prototype flew for the first time in January 1939. Its shoulder-wing configuration and tricycle undercarriage were relatively new conceptions, but testing trials indicated a great potential future for the design and, after many minor modifications, the first operational Mitchells were issued to the 17th Bombardment Group, in mid-1941. After America's entry into the global war, a Mitchell was the first American twin-engined bomber to sink a Japanese

submarine – on 24 December 1941. On 18 April 1942, led by Colonel 'Jimmy' Doolittle, 16 Mitchells took off from the deck of the USS Hornet, flew some 800 miles across Pacific waters, and bombed Tokyo and other Japanese mainland cities. This feat of arms gained international acclaim, and Doolittle was awarded a Congressional Medal of Honor. In March 1942 deliveries of Mitchells commenced to Russia, eventually totalling 870 aircraft; the first deliveries to the RAF began in 1941, and the first RAF operational Mitchell squadrons, Nos 98 and 180, began operations with the type on 22 January 1943. More than 800 Mitchells saw eventual RAF use, equipping a total of eight squadrons, apart from training units. In USAAF use the Mitchell, in successively modified variants, gave sterling service in the Pacific area until the end of the war, mainly as a low-level attack bomber and strafer. The most widely produced variant was the B-25J, of which 4318 were built, and this version carried no less than 13 half-inch calibre machine guns in addition to a bomb load of 3-4000 lb, the latter depending on range required to target.

There is an example at Duxford.

NORTH AMERICAN MUSTANG

Considered by many ex-fighter pilots as the best all-round fighter of World War II, the Mustang – originally titled NA-73 by its manufacturers, and known as the P-51 to the USAAF – was initially designed and produced for purchase by the British. The first production example, AG345, was completed on 16 April 1941, and the second aircraft, AG346, arrived in Britain in October 1941 for test and RAF evaluation. Rejected by Fighter Command due to poor high-altitude performance, the first Mustang to enter RAF squadron use went to 26 Squadron in January 1942, ostensibly for army co-operation duties. The Mustang's first operational sortie came on 10 May 1942, flown by AG418 of 2 Squadron, and the type remained in limited first-line use by the RAF until the cessation of hostilities in May 1945, mainly in the tactical reconnaissance support role, in which it performed well. Though little interested in the design in its early days, the USAAF ordered some 500 examples after the USA came into the war, and these were first employed operationally from mid-1943 in the North African campaign. Meanwhile attempts to improve the overall fighting performance of the original Allison-engined design led to the installation of Packard-built Rolls Royce Merlin 61 engine, and the first example thus modified (AL975) immediately proved far superior for pure combat roles. Merlin-engined Mustangs entered service operationally from UK bases from December

1943, and its hugely successful combat career escalated swiftly in the hands of many of the top-scoring American fighter pilots. Continuing modification eventually enabled Mustangs to escort their USAAF bomber charges both to and from distant targets in Germany, while in the Far and Middle East war zones other Mustangs maintained an equally high operational reputation. By August 1945 the USAAF had some 5500 Mustangs on charge overall, while the RAF held another 1300 in service. Postwar production of the design continued in Australia, and both American and Australian Mustang units saw

further operations during the early years of the Korean conflict. At least 24 RAF squadrons had been equipped with Mustangs at some period, while its extensive use by the USAAF in the 1944-45 period alone ensures the Mustang a worthy place in fighter history.

There is an example at Duxford.

REPUBLIC P-47 THUNDERBOLT

Renowned in its day as the biggest and heaviest single-seat fighter ever built, the P-47 quickly earned such nicknames as 'T-Bolt' and, more commonly, 'Jug' (after Juggernaut). Flown in prototype form originally on 6 May 1941, the Thunderbolt first entered USAAF service with the 56th Fighter Group in November 1942, shortly before this Group arrived in England for active service. Operations began on 8 April 1943, mainly in the high escort role protecting the Eighth Air Force's B-17 and B-24 bomber formations to Germany. Subsequent modification increased the Thunderbolt's effective range, enabling P-47 squadrons to roam far and wide over enemy territory, where its unequalled diving speed and rugged construction made it a formidable foe to the Luftwaffe. In pure fighter combat many of the USAAF's leading fighter 'aces', such as Gabreski, Johnson and Schilling, all flew P-47s when accumulating their victory tallies. Thunderbolts also saw service in the Pacific with Australian-based USAAF units, while the type entered RAF service in the Burma campaign from September 1944 and equipped a total of 16 RAF squadrons in that war theatre. Weighing some 17,500 lb fully war-loaded, yet capable of attaining more than 400 mph at an altitude of 30,000 feet, the P-47, with its six or eight wing-mounted .50 inch calibre machine guns was the equal of any piston-engined fighter of its day. Between April 1943 and August 1945, Thunderbolts flew more than half a million operational missions, during which they expended more than 135 million rounds of ammunition, 60,000 rockets, and claimed nearly five enemy aircraft destroyed for every P-47 lost in action.

The example illustrated is one of several airworthy examples still flown by the self-styled 'Confederate Air Force' based in the USA.

SHORT SUNDERLAND

The background to the Sunderland's outstanding service began in November 1933, when Air Ministry issued AM Specification R.2/33, calling for a four-engined, long-range, reconnaissance flying boat to replace the existing biplane flying boats in RAF squadrons. Short Brothers decided to produce a military version of a civil flying boat then under construction, the C-class, intended for Imperial Airways (forerunner

of the present British Airways). On 16 October 1937 the first-ever Sunderland (K4774) was launched at Rochester, Kent; the first Sunderland to enter RAF service (L2159) arrived at Seletar, Singapore on 22 June 1938 and joined 230 Squadron. By September 1939 only three squadrons were equipped but by August 1945 a total of at least 20 squadrons had flown Sunderlands. Used primarily in the anti-submarine and convoy escort roles, Sunderlands were responsible for sinking at least 37 U-boats and seriously damaging some 21 others; but their greatest contribution to the air-sea war was as a 'deterrent', acting as a constant threat to German and Italian submarines. Other duties included many mercy missions, such as retrieving Allied troops from Crete and Greece during evacuations, and picking up wounded and sick troops from behind Japanese lines in Burma. Occasionally, Sunderland captains even landed in open waters attempting to rescue ditched air crews, despite the fact that the aircraft was never designed for such harsh treatment. Early clashes with Luftwaffe fighters gave Sunderland air gunners some victories, and led to the German nickname for the Sunderland of *Stachelschwein* ('Porcupine'), referring to its four gun positions for defence. Full production of the design, which amounted to 739 aircraft, ceased in June 1946, but Sunderlands remained in RAF service and played important roles in the Berlin Airlift, Malayan campaign, Korean War, and other minor circumstances. On 20 May 1959 Sunderland ML797 of 205 Squadron, Seletar made the final sortie by a Sunderland in RAF livery.

The photo shows Sunderland GR5, ML824 which saw brief operational war service with 201 and 330 Squadrons, and which now resides in its former 201 Squadron markings at the RAF Museum, Hendon.

SUPERMARINE SPITFIRE

Bearing a name that has become an international legend in fighter aircraft history, the Spitfire was the brainchild of Reginald J Mitchell, Supermarine's chief designer who had been responsible for, among others, the successful S-series of racing floatplanes which secured for Britain permanent possession of the Schneider Trophy in 1931. The prototype, K5054, first took to the air on 5 March 1936, and within weeks the Air Ministry placed its first production contract with its makers. First to receive Spitfires as re-

equipment was 19 Squadron at Duxford in July 1938, and within a year a further eight squadrons had also received Spitfires or were in the process of re-equipping. Throughout the war of 1939-45 the Spitfire remained the *only* Allied fighter to be continuously produced, during which period the design increased its engine power by 100 per cent, its top speed by some 40 per cent, its rate of climb by 80 per cent, and its loaded weight by 40 per cent. Spitfires were flown by every Allied air force, in virtually every operational theatre and role. In all more than 22,000 Spitfires (including

the naval Seafire variants) were built before production ceased in late 1947. This total included more than 40 major variants, and a host of minor modified versions for specific roles; an overall indication of the tremendous built-in development potential of Mitchell's original design. Added to its unsurpassed fighting reputation was a beauty of line which led the distinguished artist Sir William Rothenstein to describe the Spitfire '...as pretty and as precious-looking as a cavalier's jewelled rapier'.

A number of Spitfires, of various Marks, still exist, including airworthy examples such as AR501 (illustrated). This Spitfire saw wartime service with 310 (Czech) Squadron, whose markings it now wears, and later served with 504 and 312 Squadrons, apart from several training units. It belongs to the Shuttleworth Trust and is based at Duxford, from where it flies regularly at various public displays.

SUPERMARINE WALRUS

Known initially as the Seagull V, the Walrus amphibian design was originally produced to a Royal Australian Air Force requirement for an aircraft amphibian which could be catapulted from a warship, fully loaded, and be capable of performing naval reconnaissance duties. The first example made its maiden flight on 21 June 1933 from Southampton Water, but it was not until May 1935 that the Air Ministry placed a contract for production for the Fleet Air Arm of 12 machines. In August that year the design's name was officially changed to Walrus, though its unofficial nickname of 'Shagbat' became universally adopted in later years. The Seagull V, incidentally, was the first *military* aircraft in the UK to incorporate a fully retractable undercarriage. As production steadily increased, examples of the Walrus began to be used on many of the Fleet's battleships and aircraft carriers. When war came in 1939 a number of Walrus aircraft were placed on RAF charge, and from late 1941 these became an invaluable facet of the burgeoning Air-Sea Rescue Service. Despite their extreme vulnerability, Walrus ASR crews often flew perilously close to enemy shores in their attempts to rescue ditched Allied air crews, often alighting in mine-strewn seas in their determination to retrieve their comrades. Such courage was directly responsible for saving the lives of several hundred Allied airmen, and preventing their capture by German forces. FAA Walrus crews saw extensive operational service in many war zones, but, like their RAF counterparts in the ASR Service, received very little recognition of their sterling work. Total production ceased in January 1944, by which date 741 Walrus aircraft had been built.

Walrus I, L2301 (pictured) is now with the Fleet Air Arm Museum at Yeovilton.

VICKERS WELLINGTON

With its contemporaries the Armstrong Whitworth Whitley and the Handley Page Hampden, the Vickers Wellington bore the heavy responsibility of carrying the air war to Germany during the first three years of World War II, before succeeding four-engined bombers were available in sufficient quantity for use on RAF operations. Known affectionately to its crews as 'Wimpy' (after J Wellington Wimpy, a Popeye cartoon strip character of the pre-1939 era), the Wellington incorporated geodetic style construction and first flew in prototype (K4049) on 15 June 1936. The first production Wellington was issued to 9 Squadron at Mildenhall in October 1938, and by the beginning of the war a year later a further nine squadrons were fully-or part-equipped. The Wimpy commenced its operational career on the first day of the war, and continued to make a large contribution to the day and night bombing offensive against Germany until the ultimate bombing sortie on 8 October 1943. Thereafter Wellingtons continued on operations from the UK with Coastal Command, accounting for at least 51 U-boats sunk or seriously damaged. In the Middle East Wellingtons added lustre to the type's fighting record from 1940 until early 1945;

while from 1943 Wellingtons joined the war in India and Burma as night bombers. At one time or another Wellingtons were flown by at least 76 RAF or Allied Air Forces' squadrons, apart from its wide use late in the war for crew training. Total production of all variants of Wellington amounted to 11,461, the last machine being delivered from the Squires Gate factory at Blackpool on 13 October 1945.

The sole surviving example is MF628, a Mk X, built in 1944 and, after a chequered career, handed over to the RAF Museum, Hendon on 26 October 1971, where it may be viewed today.

WESTLAND LYSANDER

Designed specifically for army co-operation duties, the Lysander – inevitably, 'Lizzie' to her crews – first flew in June 1936, and entered RAF service with 16 Squadron at Old Sarum, Wiltshire in June 1938. Though relatively slow – its maximum speed was little better than 200 mph – and with light defensive armament of three machine guns, the Lysander saw service in France during 1939-40 and was responsible for shooting down the first Heinkel bomber in BEF territory, in November 1939. Used primarily for artillery spotting, general reconnaissance, and supply dropping, the Lizzie also served in the early campaigns in the Middle East in 1939-41, before relinquishing its role to more modern, faster aircraft. In the UK the type survived on active service thereafter as a general target-towing trainer and gunnery instruction machine, but saw its widest use as part of the burgeoning air-sea rescue organisation covering British coastal waters; a role in which it was part-responsible for retrieving hundreds of ditched air crews from the sea. A lesser-known but vital role filled by some Lysander crews was the 'Special Duties' organisation, wherein specially adapted Lysanders, with long-range fuel tank under the fuselage and side ladder attached to the rear cockpit, flew spies and 'special agents' in and out of German and French territories by night. In this guise Lysanders of 138 and 161 Squadrons completed at least 400 'SD' sorties betweer 1941 and 1944.

Illustrated is Lysander III, R9125, LX-L, marked

in the code letters of 225 Squadron, 1940, to which unit it was first issued. It now resides in the RAF Museum, Hendon.

APPENDIX

United Kingdom Aviation Museums & Collections

Over the past 60 years interest in the preservation and restoration of historic aircraft has steadily increased, not only in Britain but on an international scale. Indeed, the last 20 years have witnessed a rapidly mushrooming 'industry' in this context, including a variety of specially manufactured replica aircraft based on the past classic aircraft designs. The following tabulation should not be regarded as comprehensive, but does list a majority of the principal aviation 'museums' for those especially interested in viewing vintage aircraft and associated impedimenta. It is emphasised, however, that many are privately owned; hence it may be taken as a necessary pre-requisite that intending visitors *must write first* to the addresses given, whence full details of permitted visiting hours and dates may be ascertained. Equally, where RAF or other Service establishments are listed, it is *always* necessary first to contact, *by letter*, the appropriate officer commanding.

Aeroplane Collection Ltd
8 Greenfield Avenue, Urmston,
Manchester M31 1XN

Airborne Forces Museum
Officer Commanding,
Browning Barracks, Aldershot,
Hampshire GU11 2DS

Aircraft Preservation Society of
Scotland
28 Weavers Knowe Crescent,
Currie EH14 5PL

Birmingham Museum of
Science & Technology
Newhall Street,
Birmingham B3 1RZ

Bristol City Museum
Queens Road, Clifton,
Bristol BS8 1RL

British Rotorcraft Museum
Delta House, Summer Lane,
Worle, Weston-super-Mare,
Avon BS22 OBE

Cornwall Aero Park
Culdrose Manor, Helston,
Cornwall TR13 OGA

Cosford Aerospace Museum
Officer Commanding,
RAF Cosford,
Wolverhampton,
West Midlands WV7 3EX

Durney Aeronautical Collection
276 Weyhill Road, Andover,
Hampshire

Duxford Imperial War Museum,
Duxford Airfield, Duxford,
Cambridgeshire CB2 4QR

East Anglian Aviation Society
37 Stirling Road, St Ives,
Huntingdon,
Cambridgeshire PE17 4UU

Glasgow Museum of Transport
25 Albert Drive,
Glasgow G41 2PE

Humberside Aviation Museum
Elsham Country Park, Brigg,
South Humberside DN33 3BZ

Imperial War Museum
Lambeth Road, London SE1 6HZ

Lashendon Air Warfare Museum
Headcorn Aerodrome, Headcorn,
Kent TN27 9HX

Merseyside Aviation Society Ltd
16 Walsingham Road,
Liverpool L16 3NT

Midland Air Museum
c/o Coventry Airport, Baginton,
Warwickshire

R J Mitchell Hall
Kingsbridge Lane, Southampton,
Hampshire SO1 OGB

R J Mitchell Memorial
Bethesda Road, Hanley,
Stoke-on-Trent

Mosquito Aircraft Museum
Salisbury Hall, London Colney,
St Albans, Hertfordshire

Museum of Army Flying
Officer Commanding,
Army Air Corps Centre,
Middle Wallop, Stockbridge,
Hampshire SO20 8DY

Museum of Flight
Royal Scottish Museum,
East Fortune Airfield,
North Berwick,
East Lothian EH39 5LF

Newark Air Museum
141 Hawton Road,
Newark NG24 4QG

Norfolk & Suffolk Aviation
Museum
c/o 46 Lockhart Road, Ellingham,
Bungay, Suffolk NR35 2HB

Northumbrian Aeronautical
Collection
91 Toner Avenue, Hebburn,
Tyne & Wear NE31 2QS

Nostell Aviation Museum
15 Troon Road, Hatfield,
Doncaster, South Yorkshire

Personal Plane Services Ltd
Wycombe Air Park, Marlow,
Buckinghamshire

Royal Air Force Museum (inc.
Battle of Britain Museum)
The Hyde, Hendon,
London NW9 5LL

RAF St Athan Museum
Officer Commanding,
RAF St Athan,
Barry, Glamorgan CF6 9WA

**RAF Battle of Britain Memorial
Flight**
Officer Commanding,
RAF Coningsby,
Lincoln LN4 4SY

**Royal Navy, Fleet Air Arm
Museum**
Officer Commanding,
RNAS Yeovilton,
Somerset BA22 8HT

Science Museum
Exhibition Road,
South Kensington,
London SW7 2DD

Shuttleworth Collection
The Aerodrome, Old Warden,
Biggleswade, Bedfordshire

Skyfame Aircraft Museum
Staverton Airport, Cheltenham,
Gloucestershire

Strathallan Aircraft Collection
Strathallan Airfield,
Auchterarder,
Perthshire PH3 1LA

Thorpe Water Park
Leisure Sport Ltd
Eastley End House,
Coldharbour Lane, Thorpe,
Egham, Surrey TW20 8TD

Torbay Aircraft Museum
Higher Blagdon, Paignton,
Devon TQ3 3TG

Wales Aircraft Museum
Hafod-y-Bryn, 72 New Road,
Llanelli, Dyfed SA14 8QQ

**Yorkshire Aircraft Preservation
Society**
49 Dales Walk, Stamford Bridge,
North Humberside